THE KING PENGUIN BOOKS

* 75 *

MONUMENTAL BRASSES

MONUMENTAL BRASSES

BY

JAMES MANN

WITH THIRTY-TWO
PLATES

PENGUIN BOOKS · MCMLVII

THE KING PENGUIN BOOKS

EDITOR: N. B. L. PEVSNER
PUBLISHED BY PENGUIN BOOKS LTD
HARMONDSWORTH, MIDDLESEX, ENGLAND
TEXT PAGES PRINTED BY
R. AND R. CLARK LTD, EDINBURGH
COLOUR PLATES MADE AND PRINTED BY
JOHN SWAIN AND SONS LTD, BARNET
COVER DESIGNED BY JOHN GRIFFITHS
MADE IN GREAT BRITAIN
FIRST PUBLISHED
1957

Foreword

MONUMENTAL BRASSES form a much larger subject than is usually covered by a King Penguin.

This little book can be no more than an introduction to an important branch of Medieval Art, about which a great many books have been written. Though constrained to treat the subject in a small compass, I have allowed myself a little more scope to deal with one or two aspects which other writers have overlooked or where they have been misled. I have tried here to show the enduring connexion between the monumental effigy sculptured in the round and the brass engraved in the flat.

Many writers have misused the proper terms for describing armour and costume, as their knowledge of these subjects was limited to the evidence offered by the brasses themselves. This has led to many errors of interpretation. What is shown in purely linear form on brasses must also be seen in the light shed by the other arts, and can only be properly understood by a first hand knowledge of what they were intended to portray. I have also given space to discussion of those old fables 'banded' mail and the cross-legged attitude.

Plates 4 and 5, 8B, 9, 10, 12, 15B and D, 19, 20, 22, 24 and 25, 28, 30, and 31 were drawn specially for this volume by Mr Theodore Ramos, and Plates 19 and 32 by Miss Elizabeth Grant; Plates 1, 2, 3, 8A, 11, 13, 14, 15C, 16, 21, 23, 26, 27, and 29 have been taken from the brothers L. A. B. and J. G. Waller's *A Series of Monumental Brasses from the Thirteenth to the Sixteenth Centuries*; Plates 6, 7, 15A, 17, and 18 are based on R. B. Utting's woodcuts in the Rev. Charles Boutell's *A Series of Monumental Brasses in England*; the decoration on the title-page and the tailpiece on page 36 are from Herbert Haines's *A Manual of Monumental Brasses*.

To meet the small format of this book inscriptions and in some cases canopies have been omitted from some of the plates in order that the essential parts can be reproduced on a larger scale.

In conclusion, I should like to thank my friends Mr R. H. D'Elboux, F.S.A., Vice-President of the Monumental Brass Society, and Mr J. L. Nevinson for kindly reading the manuscript of this book and for many valuable comments thereon.

J. G. M.

Monumental Brasses

THE MONUMENTAL BRASS, engraved on one or more flat bronze plates, corresponds closely to the contemporary stone monument with its effigy sculptured in the round.

There are more monumental brasses in England than in all the other countries of Europe combined, and the English brass shows distinctive characteristics of its own. It is calculated that some 10,000 examples survive in this country out of what once must have been a very large total. They have been reduced in number by the religious upheavals of the Reformation, by metal thieves, vandalism, and neglect.

A third form of memorial is the incised slab of stone. This can be regarded as the parent from which the other two have sprung. The incised slab derives from the stone lid which covered the coffin and was at first carved with an inscription or ornament, then with a portrayal of the deceased in outline. It was further enhanced by raising the design in relief, and from this came the figure carved in the round. The brass is in effect the incised slab translated to a more durable material in which artistic details could be precisely rendered. Stone slabs incised with human figures are not very common in England but exist in considerable numbers abroad.

Our knowledge of the early history of memorial brasses has been much obscured by the destruction of family monuments on the Continent, and especially in France during the Revolution of 1789. The earliest existing brass is that of Bishop Yso Wilpe at Verden near Hanover, d. 1231 (Plate 32). All evidence combines to indicate the Low Countries as the place of origin of engraved brasses as personal memorials.

The bronze plates were made of 'laton' or 'latten', an alloy of copper and zinc, with a little lead and tin. It was much used in the Middle Ages. Utensils, both religious and secular, were cast from it, statuettes, tabernacles, and so forth, and, on a larger scale, screens and lecterns. The plates of which brasses are composed are not large, measuring from 2 feet 6 inches to 3 feet square. The engraved plates were inserted in stone slabs, often of Purbeck 'marble', cut to receive them (indents). They were fixed by being laid in pitch and, all except a few early ones, secured by brass pins made flush with the surface. The slabs when still in their original positions in the church usually cover the body of the deceased. The design and engraving of the vast majority of brasses in England were certainly carried out in this country.

There is a marked difference in style and composition between the English brass and the Continental variety, and it is easy to distinguish from internal evidence the sixteen or so brasses of Continental workmanship that have found their way into English churches (see p. 34). The strong and confident lines of English brasses of the best period serve as a corrective to an old tendency to attribute English works of art to foreign sources if they happen to have special merit.

Who were responsible for the work? The beautiful gilt bronze effigies of King Henry III and Queen Eleanor in Westminster Abbey, cast by the *cire-perdue* method, are known from the evidence of a Close Roll to be the work of William Torel, goldsmith of London in 1291. The goldsmiths were a large guild and worked in many metals besides gold. But the masons, too, have a strong claim, borne out by a mark on the brass of Lady Creke, *c.* 1325, at Westley Waterless in Cambridgeshire (Plate 3) which corresponds closely with the extant seal of a certain Walter le Masun. Both show within a circle the letter N beneath a mallet, with a moon and star on either side.

Further evidence of masons participating in the production of brasses is provided by wills of the fifteenth century. The brasses of the late sixteenth century at West Firle in Sussex are known from documentary evidence to be the work of Gerard Johnson or Jansen, one of a family of Protestant refugees from the Low Countries (Plate 12). He founded a business in Southwark, which produced many large sculptured alabaster tombs. Edward Marshall, pupil of Nicholas Stone, who made monuments and also executed the stone pedestal of the statue of Charles I in Whitehall, signed with his name the brass of Sir Edward Filmer, 1629, and his wife in East Sutton Church, Kent, which is a rectangular engraved brass plate (Plate 13).

The theory put forward by Herbert Haines that brasses derived from Limoges enamels was based on the copper plaque enamelled in colours of Geoffrey Plantagenet, d. 1149, father of Henry II of England, preserved at Le Mans. But its size is quite small, only 25 by 13 inches. More closely akin to brasses is the engraved metal sheathing of the oak effigy of William de Valence, d. 1296, in Westminster Abbey. But this is nearly a century later than the date when brasses as we know them were already in existence.

All the earlier brasses in England show the deceased in a recumbent attitude, lying on their backs with their hands joined in prayer. Their heads rest on pillows and their feet are placed on animals, exactly as on monuments sculptured in stone. These animals were intended to obscure the upturned soles of the feet, which otherwise make an abrupt ending to the sculptured effigy. After the middle of the fourteenth century husbands are occasionally shown holding their wives' hands. The first to show the kneeling pose is the brass of John Strete, d. 1405, at Upper Hardres, Kent (Plate 28).

One must not expect to find much facial portraiture in the Middle Ages, and the faces of hundreds of brasses are as like as peas. The men are shown in the prime of life, the ladies smooth and unlined. Occasionally there are exceptions, such as Sir William Tendring, d. 1408, at Stoke-by-Nayland in Suffolk, whose bald head and long beard appear to be personal characteristics. With the spread of humanism, which came from Italy and reached England in the sixteenth century, attempts at individual portraiture increased.

The date of brasses can generally be accepted as being within a few years of the date of decease. Some were laid down in the owner's lifetime, many others were laid down by executors or widows during the lifetime of the latter, as is shown by the date of the survivor's decease being left blank, while that of the husband is duly recorded. There are several instances of testators leaving instructions for brasses to be laid down to their memory. Occasionally one finds obviously posthumous works, such as the brass of Sir John Erpingham, d. 1370, at Erpingham, Norfolk, which from the armour depicted must have been executed some fifty years later. The Stuart antiquary, Sir John Dering, set up a whole series of brasses to the memory of his ancestors in Pluckley Church, Kent. Posthumous brasses can easily be recognized by comparison with others of the supposed date.

Brasses are most commonly found in the English counties where good workable stone is scarce. The county which possesses the greatest number of brasses is Kent, and the eastern counties of Essex, Suffolk, and Norfolk are also specially rich. They are fewer in the western and northern parts of the country, where there is ample limestone and sandstone for effigies. There are only some half dozen brasses to be seen in Scotland, and five in Ireland, four of them being in Dublin.

The earliest recorded English brass, of which only the indent of a cross and inscription survives, commemorates Simon de Beauchamp, died before 1208, in St Paul's Church, Bedford. There are other indents, long stripped of their brasses, dating from the middle of the thirteenth century; two are in Salisbury Cathedral, one in Wells, and one in Westminster Abbey.

The earliest surviving brass in England is that of Sir John d'Aubernoun, d. 1277, at Stoke d'Abernon in Surrey (Plate 1). This noble figure, 6 feet long, is the first of a series which steadily increased in number after 1350 and continued well into the seventeenth century.

Most monumental brasses have as their main feature an effigy
of the deceased, and in the early examples the draughtsmanship
is firm and sure, and all unnecessary detail is eliminated. The
metal is thick, the lines engraved with a burin are deep and strong,
widening and diminishing to give them expression. Brasses of the
thirteenth and fourteenth centuries, being of thicker plate, have
as a rule stood the test of time better than their successors.

The study of monumental brasses is an excellent introduction
to medieval art. They are closely connected with developments in
contemporary architecture and sculpture. They are an important
vehicle of religious symbolism. Above all, they record inimitably
English society in the Middle Ages, the personnel of the court,
the landowners, large and small, the church, both secular and
monastic, and the legal and commercial classes of the towns.

The earliest examples, numbering only about two dozen, are
spread over three-quarters of a century (1277–1350), and are for
the most part of large size and represent people of importance.
After this the use of brasses as memorials extends socially and they
tend to become smaller in size. Small whole-length figures of
about 14 inches indicate that in the fifteenth century they were
being ordered by persons with less money to spend. After the
middle of the fifteenth century a decline in quality sets in, and
shading by hatched lines was mistakenly introduced to give the flat
linear figures the appearance of a third dimension. In brasses, as in
stone monuments, the Gothic inspiration had exhausted itself,
though it was to continue strong in architecture. During the
first half of the sixteenth century most brasses are small, inac-
curate, and badly drawn. That of Sir Thomas Bullen (Plate 11)
is a notable exception. There is a revival in the later years of
Queen Elizabeth I following the influx of refugee artists from
the Low Countries. The Civil War brought the monumental
brass with human figures virtually to an end, as it did many
other survivals of the Middle Ages.

The close mutual resemblance of certain groups of brasses
scattered about the country indicates the work of a common

workshop. The existence of details common to each other in certain brasses, otherwise unlike, increases the membership of these groups. London undoubtedly was the main centre of production, but idiosyncrasies in the drawing of brasses in certain parts of the country denote local workshops, e.g. at York in the north (Plate 9A), and there is a marked style found in East Anglia which suggests Norwich as another provincial centre (Plate 9B).

The evidence supplied by brasses is of the greatest help in the study of defensive armour in the Middle Ages. Its evolution can

Military Brasses

be roughly divided into three periods: (*a*) the age of mail, up to the fourteenth century, the last brass showing complete mail being that of Sir John Gifford, *c.* 1348, at Bowers Gifford, Essex; (*b*) the age of mail with additions of plate, with mail predominating throughout the first half of the fourteenth century and plate predominating during the second half; and (*c*) complete plate armour from about 1410 onwards. The armour of the second half of the fifteenth century is commonly described as 'Gothic', then in the course of the sixteenth century it changes radically under the influence of the Renaissance.

The earliest existing brass, as already mentioned, is that of Sir John d'Aubernoun, d. 1277 (Plate 1). He is shown wearing a hood (coif) of mail, a mail shirt (hauberk) reaching to just above the knees and with sleeves extending over the hands in the form of mittens, and mail stockings to the toes. The knees are covered by 'poleyns', probably made of moulded leather incised with decorative lines. Strapped to his feet are pointed spurs known as 'prick' spurs. Over his shirt of mail he wears a linen surcoat which is caught in at the waist with a cord. Over his right shoulder is a strap or 'guige', from which the shield carried on his left arm is suspended. His sword-belt is fastened together by an intricate system of laced thongs. His sword-hilt is cruciform, the pommel is circular and the quillons (cross guard) nearly straight. Held vertically inside his right arm is a shortened ver-

sion of his lance. His arms are *azure, a chevron or*; the blue colour
being rendered in enamel. His feet rest on a lion.

The brass of Sir Roger de Trumpington,* at Trumpington near
Cambridge (Plate 2), shows certain differences. He is using as a
pillow his great conical helm, which was worn over the mail coif.
Behind his shoulders are two rectangular additions known as ai-
lettes, engraved with his arms. They are shown thus because of
the difficulty of reproducing them in perspective in two dimen-
sions, but effigies sculptured in stone show that they were laced
to the side of the shoulders rather than behind them. Some writers
regard them as an additional defence, but it is probable that their
intention was mainly heraldic. Trumpington's shield is shown
convex, whereas that of Sir John d'Aubernoun is flat. The few
actual shields which survive from this time show that the shield
was bent to a shallow convex section (as for instance that of
the Black Prince among his 'achievements' at Canterbury Cathedral).

There are some popular fallacies that need correction. It will be
noticed that the legs of the earlier figure are straight, and of the
second crossed. The latter attitude has been assumed by many to
denote that the person represented was a Crusader. Sir Roger
did actually take the Cross as one of the retinue of Prince Edward
in 1270, but there is ample evidence that the subjects of most cross-
legged figures of both brass and stone never in their lives went to
Palestine. This has caused the adherents of this view to substitute
another suggestion, that the attitude denotes a benefactor of the
church. Both ideas are probably mistaken. Taking the long view, it
will be noted that the cross-legged attitude covers a very short period
of time in the history of engraved brasses and effigies sculptured
in stone, and that it coincides with what is called the 'Decorated

*This brass, long believed to be the second oldest in point of date
(1289), may have been laid down posthumously. The indent of a
surrounding fillet for the marginal inscription suggests the early fourteenth century, but if the brass is contemporary with Sir Roger's death
it is the earliest instance of this feature.

14 Period' in church architecture. Contemporary sculptured figures in armour on the west front of Exeter Cathedral are shown seated with crossed legs and folded arms. The taste of the time demanded variety and movement in its compositions, and eschewed the straight line. One finds the same intention with the swayed pose often given to the body (Plate 4). The last effigy (in stone) to show the posture of crossed legs is at Dorchester, Dorset, and dates from *c*. 1370. With the coming of the 'Perpendicular' period the legs are again made straight.

The convention used for representing mail (a textile of inter-linked, riveted iron rings) differs in both figures. That of Sir John d'Aubernoun takes the form of clearly defined interlocking half rings, that of de Trumpington is much simplified by showing semicircular crescents set in rows and turned in alternate directions. The latter form is even more pronounced on the brass of Sir John d'Aubernoun's son of the same name, d. 1327, also at Stoke d'Abernon, and the contemporary brass of Sir John de Creke, *c*. 1325, at Westley Waterless, Cambridgeshire (Plate 3). In their cases the rows of alternating crescents are separated by double lines, and it has been held in the past that this represents a speci-ally constructed kind of mail, called by its proponents 'banded' mail. It has been argued either that the links are threaded together with leather thongs (Waller), or that an even more elaborate sys-tem in which the rows of links are strung together and their edges covered with leather strips is indicated (Ashdown). The fact that no specific mention of these two systems exists in any written record, and that nothing of the kind has ever been found (though the excavation of true mail since Roman times is common), make it certain that both representations are a form of shorthand used to denote a highly intricate structure of thousands of rings. The word 'mail' means only one thing, interlinked rings of iron. It is unnecessary to call it chain-mail.

Sir John d'Aubernoun's feet rest on a lion and those of Trump-ington on a hound. This has been assumed to denote that one died in battle and the other in his bed. Inquiries into the lives of per-

sons so represented quickly dispose of this fallacy. The lion may
be taken as a symbol of manly courage, quite appropriate to a
knight, and the hound that of his sport, which has been called 'the
image of war without its guilt'. Incidentally, there are instances
of ladies and even of a priest with lions at their feet.

Most writers on brasses are guilty of grossly misusing the technical terms employed to describe parts of armour. Early writers
on armour, such as Meyrick and Hewitt, compiled a vocabulary
drawn at random from French and English manuscript sources,
with the result that a number of unnecessary gallicisms (*menton-
nières*, *genouillières*, etc.) have crept in where English words would
suffice. The same applies to Latin words. Again, many of the old
words have been misunderstood and misapplied. Fortunately, we
have the evidence of an early fifteenth-century description of the
brass of Sir Hugh Hastings, d. 1347, at Elsing, Norfolk (Plates 4
and 5), which was adduced as evidence in a law-suit of Grey *versus*
Hastings on the right to bear the arms shown. This makes quite
clear what were the technical terms in use at that time. Certain
words should be eschewed altogether, such as *tuile*, a word which
never existed and has arisen through a misreading of the word
toile (cloth) in Sir John Tiptoft, Earl of Worcester's *Rules for the
Tournament* of 1466. There is no difference between *taces* and
tassets, both are variant forms of the same word. Similarly the
word *pasguard* has been misunderstood as denoting the *haute-piece*
of the pauldron, when it really means a reinforcement for the
left elbow on a tilt armour; and *tapul* has been interpreted as
being the ridge down the centre of a sixteenth-century breast
plate. Its true meaning is obscure.

Though there is little doubt that the brasses of the next genera-
tion, of Sir John de Creke and Sir John d'Aubernoun II, d. 1327,
are by the same hand, there are certain significant differences in
detail. One is bearded (the new fashion) and the other clean
shaven like his immediate forebears. Both wear light, pointed
helmets known as bascinets, and both show plate additions to the
mail on the arms and on the legs. The former has little embossed

lions on the shoulders and elbows, probably made of leather, and his spurs are of the new rowel type, while d'Aubernoun's are of the prick type, which was then going out. Both wear surcoats shortened at the front, which enables one to see a succession of defences beneath. Under the surcoat is worn a defence probably made up of small plates fastened together by rivets. Below the skirt of the mail shirt can be seen the padded gambeson or wambais, which it was necessary to wear beneath mail to prevent its chafing the wearer.

Writers in the past have classified armour in periods called by such names as the 'Surcoat Period', the 'Cyclas Period', the 'Tabard Period', etc., and have quite arbitrarily attached the second of these words to the surcoat when shortened in front, as shown by the Creke and younger d'Aubernoun brasses. This is a misuse of a much older word, and it is a mistake to try and define periods of armour by so superficial a thing as a linen surcoat. The shortening of the surcoat in front was a passing fashion, which was completed by cutting short the back tails also and so producing what has been called the 'skirted' jupon, worn in the middle years of the century (Plate 4). The skirted jupon quickly lost its looseness and became the tight close-fitting jupon (or gipon) which gives an almost uniform appearance to military brasses from the sixties of the fourteenth century to about 1410 (Plates 6 and 7A). This close-fitting, sleeveless body garment often had the owner's arms embroidered on it. The pointed steel helmet known as a bascinet (basnet), was at first worn under the great helm, and later by itself. The neck and throat were protected by the pendant aventail (or camail) which was hung on staples, called vervelles, along the lower edge of the bascinet. These are clearly shown on most military brasses and effigies from the middle of the century until near the nineties, when it was covered for safety by a metal strip, often elaborately enriched. The old loose sword-belt was abandoned and replaced by an enriched baldric worn horizontally round the hips and probably supported on hooks. This is at first shown with the buckled end looped round itself, and after *c.* 1375 as a rigid band of engaged brooches. It carried the sword in a vertical position on the left hip, on the right was a dagger, which from now on becomes a universal feature. It takes different forms, the most usual being the quillon, ballock or rondel types, so named from their shapes of hilt.

For a short time between 1330 and 1370 the thighs are shown decorated with small circles (Plate 4). This has been called studded armour, or *pourpointerie* (quilting, from the Latin *perpunctum*), but in point of fact these circles represent the rivet-heads of a type of brigandine defence made up of small plates riveted to a canvas or leather foundation and faced on the front with coloured velvet.

The lower limbs were at first protected by single greaves (shin-balds) down the front of the legs, but after 1360 by close-greaves made in two parts, back and front, joined by hinges and fastened by straps or studs. The arms were similarly enclosed in tubular plates. The hands were protected with gauntlets of plate instead of mufflers of mail. Laminated plates known as sabatons covered the feet from the insteps to the pointed toes.

The brass of William de Aldeburgh, *c.* 1360, is the last to show a shield carried on the arm. This movable defence had become redundant through the increasing use of plate armour on the body. The globose profile of the sculptured effigies of the last forty years of the fourteenth century show that some kind of rigid breast-plate was worn beneath the jupon. From the middle of the fourteenth century mail becomes subsidiary to plate, though its use was never abandoned altogether. Few brasses in England portray the pointed visor which was worn at this time to protect the face. It was generally detachable, and it is understandable that on a brass or effigy the face should be shown uncovered.

For about sixty years, from about 1350 to 1410, the appearance of military brasses is almost uniform. They present a neat, symmetrical, and workmanlike appearance (Plates 6 and 7A).

About 1410 the mail aventail was covered and eventually replaced by a plate gorget (Plate 7B); the construction of this is best seen on the sculptured effigies, such as that of Sir John Fitzalan, Earl of Arundel at Arundel in Sussex. Bascinets become rounder and less pointed at the apex. Fan-shaped guards were introduced at the elbows, palettes took the place of roundels at the vulnerable armpits, and the sword-belts were worn transversely across the 'fauld' or skirt of lames, passing from a hook on the right hip to a lower level on the left. Beards and moustaches disappear by the twenties and clean-shaven faces become the rule.

In the forties the former symmetry is gradually broken up by additional reinforcements to the left (bridle) arm and less heavy armour on the right or striking arm (Plate 8A). These changes are due to developments devised by Continental armourers, especially the armourers of Milan, from whom those Englishmen who could afford it were glad to buy their armour. Heavy pauldrons were put upon the shoulders and a large reinforcement to the left elbow. The fauld is shortened, and is compensated by hanging from it a pair of plates called tassets. In the course of the second half of the fifteenth century the fauld shrinks further and the tassets correspondingly grow. John Daundelyon, d. 1445, at Margate, Kent (Plate 8A), gives a good representation of a Milanese harness of the middle years of the century.

It is futile to distinguish these changes by dynastic titles such as 'late Lancastrian' or 'Yorkist'. The process was being dictated by masters of the craft far beyond the coast of England.

We have now reached a time when a certain amount of contemporary armour exists to control our interpretation of engraved or sculptured representations. Hitherto there have only been a few detached pieces for comparison, but from now on complete armours *cap-à-pie* exist.

Milanese armour of this time is not easy to reduce to purely linear form. Certain exaggerations and inaccuracies can be excused in its representation on brasses. The fauld is often represented longer than it probably was in fact, and in some cases, as in that of Henry Paris, d. 1466, at Hildersham, Cambridge-shire, the Milanese style is not properly understood.

The bascinet was now replaced by the sallet, a light head-piece extending behind the neck, and often visored (Plate 9 A and B). A plate beaver was substituted for the gorget. The breast-plate of a single piece is now articulated and has a placate rising to a cusped point in the middle with a central ridge. This is a marked feature of the Gothic style. Gauntlets have long pointed cuffs and sabatons long points too.

The correspondence between brasses and sculptured effigies is again shown by the fact that both dispense with a helmet in the 1480's, thus showing the head bare (Plate 8B). Brasses by this time are very numerous and often quite small in size.

The old idea of a recumbent figure tends to be forgotten, and most brasses of the second half of the fifteenth century show the figures standing on little mounds with flowers on them, while their heads are still incongruously reclining on pillowed helms. The sword is now hung loosely across the body. Sometimes the pose is altered and the figures are shown in three-quarter view or kneeling.

In the last dozen years of the fifteenth century one notices the first departure from the pointed Gothic style in the rounding of the toes of the sabatons. A marked falling off in quality is shown in all brasses after about 1500. Not only are the figures badly drawn, as in the case of Sir Thomas Brooke, d. 1529, at Cobham in Kent (Plate 10), who has absurdly long legs and no neck to speak of, but the faithful depiction of contemporary armour is abandoned in favour of a vague and out-of-date convention. The old firm lines of engraving are further confused by hatching, and the metal is thinner. Certain anachronisms, such as the Gothic breast with pointed placate, are allowed to continue into the middle of the sixteenth century, although the use of this form of breast-plate had been abandoned some fifty years before. The only concessions to modernity are the high neck guards on the shoulders (*haute-pieces*) wrongly called pasguards, and the broad rounded toes of the sabatons.

This was, of course, a bad time for the tomb-maker, who often saw his work destroyed by fanatical adherents of the Reformed Faith, and many seem to have lost heart. Some of the smaller mutilations of brasses were in fact done by members of the family or incumbents. The removal of religious symbols, such as the Trinity and the Virgin and Child, might help to save them from complete destruction.

When more settled times came with the reign of Elizabeth, there was a marked revival in the design of brasses, and we begin to learn more about their authorship. The excellent brasses of Sir Edward and Lady Gage at West Firle in Sussex, d. 1569 (Plate 12), are, as already mentioned, known to have been executed by Gerard Jansen or Johnson in 1595, and similar brasses such as that of T. Hawkins, d. 1587, aged 101, at Boughton-under-Blean, Kent, are probably from the same source. They show humped pauldrons composed of overlapping lames, long peascod breastplates, and laminated tassets such as were worn at the time, and not the anachronisms of the first half of the century. George Hodges, *c*. 1630, at Wedmore, Somerset, is shown in buff coat and boots. The brass of John Arundel, d. 1633, at St Columb Major in Cornwall, shows him in a cuirassier armour with long tassets of the period. Armour virtually ceased to be worn after the first years of the Civil War, except for a helmet, and a breast and back plate.

In the majority of brasses of ladies they are shown in company with their husbands, but there are a number of single ladies, *Ladies*   including the two fine and early figures of Joan de Cobham, at Cobham in Kent (Plate 14), and Lady Camoys, at Trotton in Sussex, both *c*. 1310. They wear the flowing garments then in fashion, with a kerchief worn over the head and a wimple concealing part of the chin. These brasses can be compared with the stone effigy of Aveline, Countess of Lancaster, in

Westminster Abbey, both in respect of costume and the handling of the drapery. The same loose garments are found on Lady Creke's brass at Westley Waterless, *c.* 1325 (Plate 3), but after 1350 ladies wear a *cote-hardie*, the upper part of which fits closely to the figure and then falls to the ground in a long flowing skirt. A mantle or cloak is draped over the shoulders and is fastened in front by a cord between two bosses. The sleeves attached to the côte-hardie often have long lappets reaching from the elbow to the ground.

Kerchief and wimple disappear after 1330 and the hair is dressed in plaits gathered on either side of the face and laced with ribbons in cauls or in bosses (Plates 6 and 15A). One form is known as the *crespigne* head-dress. An unusual garment known by the modern name of the 'sideless' cote-hardie, appears about 1370 and continues far into the next century. As its name implies, it is cut away at the sides to reveal a tight-fitting garment underneath. Frequently ladies are accompanied by small pet dogs* at their feet, which are usually covered by the folds of their skirts allowing only the points of their toes to be visible.

The changes in head-dress throughout the fifteenth century are useful for dating brasses of the period (Plate 15). The caul head-dress develops into the horned head-dress, which is made by extending the bosses of hair over the ears and placing over them an embroidered kerchief. This reaches its widest extent in the 1430's (Plate 17) and then the ends curve upwards until the horns form a horseshoe almost touching each other (Plate 15B). This was succeeded by the butterfly head-dress of the 1470's and 1480's which consists of a very large transparent veil like a nun's, supported on wire (Plate 15C). Brasses of ladies wearing this head-dress are always shown turned slightly sideways in order that it should be seen for what it is.

The waist gets higher after 1410, and turned down collars are worn at the neck. Sleeves are full and gathered in at the wrist

*The dog at the feet of Lady Cassy, 1400, at Deerhurst, Gloucestershire (Plate 16), carries the name 'Terri'.

(Plate 17). After this the neckline becomes more *décolleté*, and flowered decorations on the material are often prominent features; elaborate necklaces of goldsmith's work are worn, as on the brass of Lady Say at Broxbourne in Hertfordshire (Plate 15C). With the butterfly head-dress sleeves are close-fitting again.

It is very seldom that one sees in English art the type of head-dress most closely associated in the mind of the public with the Middle Ages, namely the 'steeple' head-dress, with a veil floating from its apex. Actually, the steeple was more common in France and Flanders, and is charmingly depicted in the illuminated manuscripts of the time. The five daughters of Sir Thomas Urswyck, d. 1479, at Dagenham in Essex, show between them a variety of fashions in head-dress.

At the end of the fifteenth century, there was introduced what is called the 'gabled' head-dress, familiar to us in the drawings of Holbein (Plate 30A). At first the sides were long, but later it was shortened into a cap called the French hood (Plates 12 and 15D). Ladies of this time are often shown on brasses in heraldic dress.

Tudor ladies wear hats, puffed sleeves, hooped skirts, and farthingales in the second half of the sixteenth century (Plate 19). Lady Filmer, already mentioned (Plate 13), is dressed in the costume familiar in the portraits of Stuart times. An important innovation about the year 1600 is that of adding heels to the shoes of both men and women.

In the Middle Ages ladies are sometimes shown in the garb of widows, wearing a veil and often with a pleated *barbe* at the throat, such as the fine early brass of Eleanor de Bohun, Duchess of Gloucester, d. 1399, who is shown dressed as a 'vowess', in Westminster Abbey.

There are a few rare examples of Abbesses, among them Dame Mary Gore, Prioress of Amesbury, d. 1436, at Nether Wallop, Hampshire, and Dame Elizabeth Herwy, d. 1527, Benedictine Abbess of Elstow, at Elstow in Bedfordshire (Plate 23B), shown holding a crozier.

The earliest brasses of civilians are those of John de Bladigdone,
c. 1325, at East Wickham, Kent, and Nicholas de Aumberdene,

Civilians   c. 1350, at Taplow, Buckinghamshire, both set in the heads of floriated crosses. Richard Torryngton, d. 1356, and his wife, at Berkhampstead, Hertfordshire, are larger and hold hands.

Gentlemen as a rule wear armour, and it is interesting to note that in some family groups the father is shown in the dress of a merchant, and his son, who has risen in the social scale, in armour. Instances of this are Simon and Roger de Felbrigg at Felbrigg in Norfolk, c. 1380, and, a century later, Alderman Feld of London and his son Sir John Feld, d. 1477, at Standon in Hertfordshire. Felbrigg's son is described as having served in the wars against the heathen in Prussia, as did his contemporary, the knight in Chaucer's *Canterbury Tales* who 'In Lettowe and Prusse hadde he reised'.

The fashionable civil dress of hood, short cloak, short tight-fitting jupon, and long hose, is seldom apparent on brasses, because civilians are usually of the merchant or legal classes, and their body garments are concealed beneath long gowns. An exception is the brass of Robert Paris, d. 1408, at Hildersham in Cambridgeshire (Plate 27), who kneels with his cloak thrown back.

The furred gowns of merchants, with their hanging folds, varied little through the years. The chief changes are those of hair, namely a full beard in the fourteenth century, reduced during the reigns of Richard II and Henry IV to two small tufts on the chin (Chaucer's 'marchant with a forkyd beard') (Plate 18). Then after about 1420 come the clean-shaven faces and the hair cut in pudding-basin style (Plate 17). Beards come into fashion again in the middle of the reign of Henry VIII, that monarch himself demonstrating the change.

In the fifteenth century the sleeves are loose and full and the body garment is drawn in at the waist with a belt, and the skirt is shortened to mid-calf (Plate 17). Frequently these burgesses are shown carrying a small purse at their belts and a baselard;

this was a flat, broad-bladed civilian sword, sometimes, but doubtfully, called an 'anelace' (Plate 18). The gown lengthens towards the end of the century and the hair is worn longer and straight.

Civilians of later Tudor and Stuart times wear the heavy fur-trimmed gowns of the period, with ruffs at their necks and shoes with rounded toes in place of the pointed ones of the Middle Ages (Plate 19). The short cloak and doublet of the time are rarely seen on brasses.

In the west country there are fine brasses of rich wool merchants, as at Northleach, Gloucestershire (Plate 18), their feet resting on woolsacks.

A separate class of civilian brasses is that of the legal profession. None is earlier than the fifteenth century and most of them *Lawyers* represent judges. They wear long gowns over which is a fur-lined mantle fastened on the left shoulder, and a hood, falling in folds round the neck. A tight-fitting skull-cap or coif was worn by Justices, Sergeants at Law, and Chief Barons of the Exchequer. It can be seen on the brass of Sir John Cassy, d. 1400, at Deerhurst, Gloucestershire (Plate 16), and Sir John Juyn, Chief Justice of the King's Bench, d. 1439, at St Mary Redcliff, Bristol. Sir William Yelverton, d. 1472, wears a coif and gown over armour at Rougham, Norfolk.

There are a few examples of notaries public or scribes who are distinguishable as they wear a curious cape or hood thrown over the left shoulder. Two examples are in St Mary Tower, Ipswich, one of which shows attached to his belt the pen-case of his trade.

Children are often shown with their parents on brasses. At first perhaps one child is shown standing on a pedestal and consider-*Children* ably smaller than its parents, though not as small as later became the fashion, as on the brasses of Sir R. de Braybrook, d. 1405, and Sir Nicholas Hawberk, d. 1407, at Cobham in Kent (both obviously from the same workshop). In some cases two generations are commemorated together, father and mother, son and daughter-in-law, all standing side by side, as on the first of the Felbrigg brasses, c. 1380, mentioned above. On the brass of Richard Quartermayne at Thame, Oxfordshire, c. 1460, the son is shown below the father, exactly similar in drawing, but slightly smaller in size. It became the practice in the second half of the fifteenth century to show children on a very small scale grouped together, the sons below the father and the daughters below the mother (Plates 13 and 28). These sometimes resulted in a person being commemorated by two different brasses, firstly as a child of its parents and later on as an adult. In groups of children shown with their parents, married daughters wear head-dresses, but unmarried ones have their hair loose and hanging down their backs. Unbaptized children are shown as chrysoms in swaddling clothes (Plate 30A).

The brasses of the clergy can be divided between secular clergy and the monastic orders. The great majority of ecclesiastical
Priests   brasses are, as one might expect, of parish priests. There are three archbishops: Grenefield, Archbishop of York and Lord Chancellor, d. 1315, in York Minster; Thomas Cranley, d. 1417, Archbishop of Dublin and Warden of New College, Oxford, where he is buried; and Samuel Harsnett, d. 1631, Archbishop of York (Plate 29). There are quite a number of bishops (Plate 20).

Secular priests are as a rule shown either in Mass vestments or processional robes. The number of vestments worn increased with the rank held. The simple deacon wore a cassock or dalmatic, a priest put over the latter an alb ornamented with embroidered 'apparels' and a chasuble. The chasuble was a garment made with a hole in the centre through which the head was passed; it then hung down over the body before and behind (Plate 20). The priest also wore a stole round his shoulders, and concealed his neck in a high embroidered collar or neck-cloth known as an amice. Some are shown carrying on the right arm an embroidered maniple, a cloth used in the Communion service.

A bishop added a rochet, gloves, buskins, and a crozier, and an archbishop the pallium. Priests of the lower ranks are shown bareheaded with their tonsures in evidence. At first the episcopal mitre was low in the crown, as on the brass of Bishop Yso Wilpe (Plate 32), but it rose to a sharp point before and behind in the course of the fourteenth century. Two ribands called *infulae* depended from it at the back.

On processional occasions the clergy wore a cope (Plate 22A). This is a semicircular garment of great richness, and when placed over the shoulders as a mantle the borders hung together down the front. Many brasses show these borders richly embroidered with orphreys of saints. The evidence of brasses is supported by surviving examples, such as the Syon cope in the Victoria and Albert Museum, enriched with the beautiful embroidery in which England excelled, and known abroad as *opus Anglicanum*. Instances among brasses are the two very fine ecclesiastical brasses of 1401 and 1462 at Balsham in Cambridgeshire.

Some brasses show priests with an almuce, a fur-lined tippet, over the surplice worn for ordinary purposes (Plate 22B). Several priests carry chalices. The first example of a priestly brass is that of Laurence de St Maur, d. 1337, at Higham Ferrers in Northamptonshire, who is shown beneath a rich canopy with figures of saints in gabled tabernacles at the sides and across the top.

The Reformation reduced but did not halt the series of clergy. The last example is that of Samuel Harsnett, d. 1631, at Chigwell, Essex, already mentioned, who wears a tall bulbous mitre of the baroque period, and is bearded in the Stuart fashion, in contrast with the medieval clergy who had shaven faces.

Some of the brasses of clergy are large and fine, and indicate that they must have cost a considerable sum of money. But there are many small figures, sometimes half-figures of parish priests, and others are commemorated by inscriptions only.

Few brasses of the religious orders have survived the Reforma-

tion. Abbot de la Mare, *c.* 1370–80, is still commemorated by a
fine brass at St Albans Abbey, which was formerly a Benedictine House. The brass of Prior Nelond, d. 1433, at Cowfold in
Sussex (Plate 21), shows him in the simple garb of his Order
under an especially fine canopy containing figures of the Virgin
and Child and saints. A late example is that of John Stodely,
d. 1502, one of the Canons Regular of St Frideswide, at Over
Winchendon, Buckinghamshire. He wears a cassock, rochet, and
a plain cope.

In the chapels of the colleges of Oxford and Cambridge and in
the regions round about, are to be found most of the small number

Academic Dress

of brasses showing academic dress. Many
graduates were also priests and the cassock is
the foundation of their dress, over which was worn the gown and
hood: sometimes a tippet or a cap.

Without colour, it is difficult to distinguish degrees from the
costume shown, but these are usually given in the inscription.
There is only one brass of an undergraduate, Thomas Baker, d.
1510, student of Civil Law at All Souls College, Oxford, shown
dressed in scholar's gown and without tonsure. He is commemorated along with David Lloyde, who died on the same day,
bachelor of both Civil and Ecclesiastical Law, also in academic
dress but with tonsure. New College, Oxford, has two examples
of academic as distinct from ecclesiastical dress. The brass of
Thomas Lorkin, d. 1596, at St Mary-the-Great, Cambridge, who
was Regius Professor of Medicine, shows the heraldic arms of his
Chair, granted in the year of his death.

It is impossible in the space of this book to cover this section ade-
quately. Besides the children's brasses mentioned above, one finds

Miscellaneous Brasses

brasses of the fifteenth century in the
form of *memento mori*, in keeping with
the melancholy religious thought of the time. These are of skele-
tons (Plate 30B), either in mantles or covered in shrouds tied

above the head and below the feet. Similar cadavers were carved at the same period lying on the lower stage of architectural monuments, with the body of the deceased shown again fully clothed on the stage above.

Religious scenes, besides those accompanying brasses, e.g. the Pietà, the Resurrection, the Trinity, the Soul being borne aloft (Plate 4), are sometimes found alone. Among secular subjects is one of John Selwyn, d. 1587, depicted performing the feat of riding a stag before Queen Elizabeth, at Walton-on-Thames, Surrey. Some articles of trade are shown, as the gloves which accompany the inscription to Peter Denot, glover, c. 1440, at Fletching in Sussex (Plate 31B). An elaborate heart-brass, showing the sacred heart with inscribed scrolls issuing from it, is of Thomas Smyth, vicar, d. 1433, at Margate in Kent (Plate 31A). A number of ecclesiastical brasses consist of chalices by themselves.

Brasses provide very useful evidence for the study of medieval heraldry or 'armory'. Not only are the arms of the principal

Heraldry on Brasses shown, but those of his wife, separately or impaled, and other alliances. Occasionally, where the deceased were connected by blood or by service to the Crown, the Royal arms are portrayed. Sir Simon Felbrigg carries the Royal Standard with the arms of St Edward impaling the quartered arms of France and England. Bishops have the shields of arms of their sees as well as their own. The Trinity is denoted by a shield-shaped composition, with triple bands of inscription radiating from the centre (Deus) to the three corners (Pater, Filius, and Sanctus Spiritus), and surrounded by an inscribed border (Plate 21). Merchants show the arms of their guilds as well as their personal trade marks, the arms of the City of London, and the Staple of Calais (Plate 28).

In some brasses the jupon (William de Aldeburgh at Aldborough, c. 1360) and later the tabard (John Wantele, d. 1424, Amberley) were shown in heraldic colours by gouging out the

brass and filling the sunken and hatched areas with coloured mastic.
The same process was applied to the small detached shields accompanying the figures of husband and wife. Where gold was intended, the brass surface was left and gilded; where silver was intended, an alloy of lead was inlaid and polished; and where colours, usually red, blue, or black, were required (green is rare and purple uncommon in English heraldry), a coloured composition was used. This has not stood the test of time and is seldom found in place. An exception is the brass of Sir John Clerk, d. 1539, at Thame, Oxon.

One finds good examples of heraldic costume in all three centuries, beginning with the brass of Sir Hugh Hastings, where a kind of coloured glass is inlaid (Plates 4 and 5). Sir John Say, d. 1473, who was Speaker of the House of Commons in the Wars of the Roses, at Broxbourne in Hertfordshire, wears a tabard of his arms, and his wife a heraldic mantle once rich with gold, red, and blue chevrons, and above there is a fine 'achievement' of his arms still retaining much of its colour.

After 1490 brasses showing heraldic tabards become common and ladies have heraldic mantles, which one may assume they seldom wore. A fine heraldic trio are Thomas Fyndorne, John, Lord Marney, and their joint wife, Bridget, d. 1549, side by side, formerly at Little Horkesley and now in Colchester Museum. Sir Humphrey Style, d. 1552, kneels in his tabard at Beckenham, Kent (cover).

The blue collar of SS, not a formal Order, but a mark of Lancastrian favour, is shown worn by many men of importance during the reign of that dynasty (p. 36). The letters are believed to stand for the word *Souverayne*, a motto used by John of Gaunt, the founder of the Lancastrian line, and painted upon the wooden tester of the tomb of his son, King Henry IV, in Canterbury Cathedral. In the Wars of the Roses the Yorkist party adopted by contrast a red collar ensigned with alternate suns and roses (title-page), and this is represented on brasses of the adherents of that line.

The brass of Henry Bourchier, Earl of Essex, d. 1483, at Little Easton, Essex, is a particularly good example of heraldic dress. He and his wife are both shown wearing mantles of the Garter; his head rests on a fine close helm with coloured mantling, and the blue Garter is girt about his left knee. An impressive heraldic eagle lies at the feet of both. Another K.G. in his collar and mantle is that of Sir Thomas Bullen, d. 1538, father of Queen Anne 'Boleyn', at Hever (Plate 11). The owner's crest is usually depicted on the helm, when it is used as a pillow.

The Order of the Broomcod, shown round the neck of Richard II in the Wilton Diptych in the National Gallery, is introduced into the inscription that forms the sole remaining part of the brass of Sir John Golafre, d. 1396, a member of the Royal Household, in Westminster Abbey.

Mottos and rebuses (that is to say pictorial puns on names) are frequently found on brasses (Plate 2). Personal badges are occasionally represented, such as the fetter-lock on the brass of Sir Simon Felbrigg, d. 1416, at Felbrigg, Norfolk, and the elbow pieces on the brass of Sir Humphrey Bourchier in Westminster Abbey, who was killed at the Battle of Barnet in 1471.

The first English brass, that of Sir John d'Aubernoun, shows him in a rectangular frame of double lines within which is a French

Architectural Details   inscription in Lombardic letters, each let individually into the stone. The brass of his son shows him under a canopy on shafts with pinnacles and a gable designed in the ogee curves of its period.

Canopies follow the architectural fashion of the day, and those of the second half of the fourteenth century exhibit the slender aspiring lines of the perpendicular style. Usually figures are shown under a single canopy, but in very grand cases the canopy is triple, e.g. the Swinbornes, father and son, d. 1391 and 1412, of Little Horkesley, Essex, the Duchess of Gloucester, d. 1399, in Westminster Abbey. Prior Nelond (Plate 21) has an especially fine perpendicular canopy. The fine English brass of Robert

Hallum, Bishop of Salisbury, d. 1417, at Constance, where he
died, shows him beneath a double canopy with figures of saints
in niches up the shafts, and the whole set within a rectangular
marginal inscription (Plate 20).

In the second half of the fifteenth century canopies become
rarer, and when portrayed, tend to lose their clean lines. The
groined interior of the canopy is sometimes introduced with poor
effect. The crockets and fillings of the lunettes are often coarsely
rendered, as in the case of John, Lord Strange, d. 1479, engraved c. 1509, and his wife at Hillingdon in Middlesex, a late
example.

The classic example of such subsidiary figures is the brass of
Sir Hugh Hastings, d. 1347, at Elsing, Norfolk (Plates 4 and 5),
which is probably of Continental origin. The larger overall
expanse of the Continental brass made such details a feasible
practice, and is referred to later.

Founders are sometimes shown with their church, chapel, or
college in their hands. An early example of this practice is the
brass of Sir John Cobham, laid down c. 1365, founder of the college at Cobham, in Kent. In the case of Judge Brian Roucliff,
d. 1494, and his wife at Cowthorpe, Yorkshire, husband and wife
carry the whole church between them.

In some cases the figure of the deceased is placed on a bracket
supported by a single shaft, or on pairs of arches. Sometimes the
whole figure, the half figure, or only the head, is set in the centre
of a floriated cross. In the case of John Strete, Rector, at Upper
Hardres in Kent, d. 1405 (Plate 26), the priest kneels at the foot,
with a prayer on a scroll passing from his hands and entwining the
shaft of the bracket on which stand the figures of St Peter and
St Paul. Some brasses take the form of a cross by itself, without
any human representation, as at Cassington, Oxfordshire, of 1414.

Many important brasses are laid on top of stone (of Purbeck
marble type) tomb-chests or altar-tombs. These are either free
standing as formerly at Little Horkesley, Essex (Sir Robert and
Sir Thomas Swinborne, 1391 and 1412), and of the Wadhams

at Ilminster, Somerset. Others are placed in stone-canopied wall recesses or Easter Sepulchres, the brass being placed either upright on the wall or horizontally. The famous and splendidly carved fourteenth-century monument to Lady Percy in Beverley Minster originally contained the brass figure of Lady Percy herself, but this is now missing. The brasses of Sir Thomas de Beauchamp, Earl of Warwick, d. 1401, and his wife, at Warwick, are now mural, but formerly lay on top of a tomb-chest under a flat tester raised on four shafts.

The inscriptions of early brasses were in Lombardic letters set individually in the stone slab (Plates 1 and 14), the language *Inscriptions* used being Norman French. The last inscription in this language is that of two men in armour, both named Robert Morle, d. 1410 and 1415 respectively, at Stokenchurch in Buckinghamshire. From the mid fourteenth century onwards inscriptions are engraved in miniscule or black-letter on strips of brass (Plate 6).

Latin is the usual language of the second half of the fourteenth century and throughout the fifteenth century. The formal wording contains many abbreviations. For instance, the frequent closing phrase, *Cujus animae propicietur deus, amen*, is shortened to *Cui. aie. ppict' ds. Am.* When the inscription is placed on a rectangular marginal fillet, the corners are usually decorated with the symbols of the four Evangelists, each with a scroll, the angel for St Matthew, the winged lion for St Mark, the winged bull for St Luke, and the eagle for St John (Plate 29). In the case of smaller brasses the inscription is generally engraved on a rectangular plate at the foot. Other variations are too numerous to mention here. There are many memorials that consist of an inscribed plate only. The first wording in English occurs on a brass of Sir Thomas and Lady Walch, 1393, at Wanlip in Leicestershire. In the course of the sixteenth century medieval miniscule lettering is replaced by Roman. In the seventeenth and into the eighteenth centuries one finds pleasing examples of cursive script. The use

of brass for engraved inscriptions has, of course, continued to
the present day and is outside the scope of this little book.

It is sometimes found when a brass is taken up from its slab, that part of an earlier brass is engraved on the back, showing that it has been turned over and re-used. In this way some very interesting fragments of earlier brasses have been preserved. For instance, there is part of a rare figure of a cross-legged knight at Clifton Campville in Staffordshire, *c.* 1310, on the other side of which is a lady of *c.* 1360. At Constantine in Cornwall, on the reverse of a brass to a member of the Jervys family, d. 1574, and his wife, there are portions of a fine Continental military brass of the fourteenth century.

Palimpsests

Undoubtedly many other discoveries of this kind remain to be made, but one would not advise a wholesale lifting of brasses, which are better left *in situ*.

The objectionable practice of robbing brasses seems to have been particularly common in the sixteenth century, when they were lifted wholesale and often re-used. The metal has always had its value. A flagrant example is the brass of Humphrey Oker, d. 1538, and his wife at Okeover in Staffordshire. Here a brass of 1447 has been bodily appropriated. Humphrey had only one wife, so the second wife from the old brass has been turned over, and eight sons and five daughters engraved and named upon the back of it. There are a few instances where old brasses have been re-engraved on their obverses to bring them up to date.

The most usual method of reproducing a monumental brass is to make a rubbing of it on white paper with cobblers' black heel-ball. The ordinary lining paper used by paper hangers, if it is of good quality, serves the purpose, except that it is normally only 22 inches wide. As this is not enough to cover the breadth of many brasses, paper of a greater width can and should be obtained.

Copying Brasses

The surface of the brass should first be wiped clean of grit and

C

dust. The paper is then unrolled over the brass and must be kept firmly in place. Brasses on walls are a problem and require powers of endurance. The rubber is advised to take a friend with him to take turns at holding and rubbing. Adhesive tape may serve, but may also leave objectionable marks on the walls. In all cases the permission of the incumbent must be sought beforehand.

It is essential when rubbing that all the detached details of the brass should be kept in their proper relation to each other. Key points should, therefore, be carefully recorded. When mounted on calico the rubbing is not easy to roll, and it is better to mount on some kind of stiffened linen or tracing paper which rolls easily. Some purists object to mounting of any kind, but this usually prevents the whole composition being seen.

Ingenious attempts have been made to produce a positive instead of a negative rubbing by using a bronze-coloured wax on black or grey paper. A washleather dabber coated with powdered graphite and applied to tissue paper is preferred by some experts, but the result is faint.

The most complete collection of rubbings of English brasses is that in the possession of the Society of Antiquaries of London. Another rich collection, and publicly accessible, is that in the Department of Engravings and Design in the Victoria and Albert Museum. Good collections also exist at the British Museum, the Archaeological Museum at Cambridge, and the Ashmolean Museum at Oxford.

There is not room to do more than touch on the subject of foreign brasses. But by reason of the existence of some sixteen or so *Foreign Brasses* important examples in England, they require mention. It is calculated that there are between 600 and 700 brasses on the Continent, mostly in Belgium, Holland, Germany, and Poland. There is a particularly fine one to King Eric Menved and his Queen Ingeborg at Ringsted in Denmark, d. 1319. This and other Flemish brasses bear a strong resemblance to certain foreign brasses in England, and must have

come from the same workshop. Two specially fine ones are at
King's Lynn (Plates 24 and 25). One represents Adam de
Walsokne, d. 1349, who, when Mayor of that city, entertained
three kings at his table, and the brass includes a representation of
the peacock feast. Another splendid example is that of Abbot
Thomas de la Mare at St Albans Abbey, of c. 1370–80.

These great brasses are each composed of a complete rectangle
of plates set edge to edge, and the whole expanse allows of much
detail; canopies with rich tabernacle work, numerous saints,
inscriptions, and Gothic decorations. The result is one of great
elaboration consistent with the Gothic style of Flanders. The
English custom of dispensing with a background accords with
that simplicity and directness found in nearly all branches of
English medieval art.

Not all foreign brasses are made in this way. The French brass
of Sir Robert de Septvans, d. 1306, at Chartham in Kent, that
of a Northwood, c. 1330, at Minster, Isle of Sheppey, and Sir
Hugh Hastings, d. 1347, at Elsing in Norfolk (Plates 4 and 5),
have figures and canopies cut out and inserted in the stone in
the English manner, as also is the case with the brass of William
Wenemaer, d. 1325, at Ghent. It is the style of their drawing and
presentation which shows their foreign origin.

Among later foreign brasses in England are those of Thomas
Pounder, d. 1525, and his wife, at St Mary Quay, Ipswich
(Plate 28), and A. Evyngar, d. 1533, and wife, at All Hallows,
Barking, London. These were engraved by competent artists,
whose names, were they known, would undoubtedly be familiar
to us in the history of pictorial art.

All these brasses used to be called Flemish. Then a distinction
was noticed and for a time some were credited to Germany;
among them the series of fine examples found in the Hansa towns
along the Baltic coast, including Lübeck, and as far as Finland.
At Nousis in that country there is a most interesting brass to the
memory of St Henry, an Englishman who accompanied an in-
vasion by the King of Sweden as missionary and was killed in

the attempt. The modern view is to return these brasses to Flemish origin, but a considerable German *œuvre* exists.

In Saxony there are important groups of brasses at Meissen and at Nordhausen. In addition, one must remember that there are large numbers of brasses in Germany cast in low relief, as in the cloisters of Mainz Cathedral; also the countless numbers of bronze '*Epitaphien*', generally consisting of a framed inscription and coat of arms, preserved in numerous German churches.

The Royal effigy of Duke Christopher, d. 1363, at Roskilde Cathedral in Denmark, shows an armed figure carved in white stone with the mail inlaid in brass engraved in the 'banded' convention. It is an interesting combination of a sculptured effigy and a brass.

It is probable that during the occupation of Normandy English-made brasses were laid down in its churches, and this would account for one or two now in French museums. Dugdale recorded a brass to the memory of John, Duke of Bedford, Regent of England and France during the minority of Henry VI, at Rouen. It had no figure, but a brass shield supported by a tree-trunk and flanked with three feathers. The drawings commissioned by the antiquary, Roger de Gaignières, of the seventeenth century, show how many monuments France lost through the Revolution. One brass, that of Bishop Jean Aventage, d. 1450, survives in the Cathedral of Amiens. There is a single brass, in the form of an altar triptych depicting the Virgin with the donor and saints, in Italy, which is now in the Cathedral of Susa near the French frontier. There is a fine brass of Flemish style at Evora in Portugal, and one of the Duke of Alcalá, d. 1571, at Seville in Spain.

Works of Reference

STEPHENSON, MILL. *A List of Monumental Brasses in the British Isles.* London, Headley Bros., 1926. Supplement by his friends Ralph Griffin and M. S. Giuseppi, 1938. (This book, the labour of a lifetime, lists in a scholarly manner all the brasses in this country known at that time.)

MACKLIN, HERBERT W. *The Brasses of England,* 1907.

Victoria and Albert Museum. *Catalogue of Rubbings of Brasses and Incised Slabs.* Classified and arranged in chronological order by Muriel Clayton; 2nd edition, Board of Education, 1929. (This is well indexed and is a useful handbook.)

WALLER, L. A. B. and J. G. *A Series of Monumental Brasses from the Thirteenth to the Sixteenth Centuries.* Drawn and engraved by J. G. Waller and L. A. B. Waller; folio, London, J. Bowyer Nichols, 1864. (A fine selection excellently drawn and reproduced, some in colour.)

The Transactions of the Monumental Brass Society from 1887 onwards, and its accompanying portfolio; edited by R. H. D'Elboux.

A full bibliography would be a long one. The early works of CHARLES BOUTELL, *Monumental Brasses and Slabs,* 1847, and *A Series of Monumental Brasses in England,* 1849, and HERBERT HAINES, *A Manual of Monumental Brasses,* 1861, are still useful. H. DRUITT'S *Costume as illustrated by Monumental Brasses,* 1906, is helpful, but is quite at sea on armour. The first writer to open up the subject was Richard Gough in his large folio volumes: *The Sepulchral Monuments of Great Britain,* 1786–1790. Craven Ord, Sir John Cullum, and the Rev. T. Cole were pioneers who rode about the country on horseback and took impressions in reverse by coating the surface of the brasses with printer's ink and then pressing paper upon them. Their example is not recommended. Their rubbings were bequeathed to the British Museum in 1834 by the antiquary Francis Douce.

Special books have been devoted to most of the counties of England, or their brasses have been catalogued in the transactions of local archaeological societies. These are given at the head of each county in Mill Stephenson's *List* mentioned above.

Index

14 – *Cobham*, Sir John Cobham, *c.* 1365: 31 – *Cobham*, Sir Nicholas Hawberk, d. 1407: 24 – *Chartham*, Sir Robert de Septvans, d. 1306: 35 – *East Malling*, Preb. Richard Adams, d. 1522: pl. 22B – *East Wickham*, J. de Bladigdone, *c.* 1325: 23 – *Hever*, Sir Thomas Bullen, K.G., d. 1538: 11, 30, pl. 11 – *Margate*, John Daundelyon, d. 1445: 18, pl. 8A – *Margate*, Thomas Smyth, d. 1433: 28, pl. 31A – *Margate*, Richard Notfelde, d. 1446 (skeleton): 27, pl. 30B – *Minster*, A Northwood, *c.* 1330: 35 – *Pluckley*, Dering monument: 10 – *East Sutton*, Sir Edward and Lady Filmer, 1629: 9, 22, pl. 13 – *Upper Hardres*, John Strete, d. 1405: 9, 31, pl. 26 – *West Malling*, Elizabeth Perepoynt, d. 1543: pl. 15D

LEICESTERSHIRE: *Wanlip*, Sir Thomas and Lady Walch, d. 1393: 32

LINCOLNSHIRE: *Laughton*, A Dalison, *c.* 1400: pl. 7A

LONDON: *Barking-by-the-Tower*, All Hallows, Andrew Evyngar, d. 1533: 35 – *Westminster Abbey*, William de Valence, d. 1296 (effigy): 9 – *Westminster Abbey*, Henry III and Queen Eleanor, 1291: 8 – *Westminster Abbey*, Aveline, Countess of Lancaster (effigy): 20 – *Westminster Abbey*, Sir John Golafre, d. 1396: 30 – *Westminster Abbey*, Eleanor de Bohun, Duchess of Gloucester, d. 1399: 22, 30 – *Westminster Abbey*, Sir Humphrey Bourchier, d. 1471: 30

MIDDLESEX: *Harrow*, Anon. civilian and wife, *c.* 1600: 24, pl. 19 – *Hillingdon*, John, Lord Strange, d. 1479 (*c.* 1509): 31

NORFOLK: *Blickling*, Anne Astley, 1512 (chrysom): pl. 30A – *Elsing*, Sir Hugh Hastings, d. 1347: 15, 31, 35, pls 4, 5 – *Erpingham*, Sir John Erpingham, d. 1370, executed *c.* 1415: 10 – *Felbrigg*, Simon and Roger de Felbrigg, *c.* 1380: 23 *Felbrigg*, Sir Simon and Lady Felbrigg, d. 1416: 28 – *King's Lynn*, Robert Braunche and wife, d. 1364: 35, pls 24-5 – *King's Lynn*, Adam de Walsokne, d. 1349: 35, pls 24-5 – *Rougham*, Sir William Yelverton, d. 1472: 24 – *Southacre*, Sir John and Lady Harsick, d. 1384: 17, pl. 6 – *Stokesby*, Edmund Clere, d. 1488: pl. 9B

NORTHAMPTONSHIRE: *Higham Ferrers*, Laurence de St Maur, d. 1337: 26

OXFORDSHIRE: *Cassington*, Roger Cheyne, 1414: 31 – *Dorchester*, Richard Bewfforest, d. 1510 (Prior): pl. 23A – *All Souls College*, Thomas Baker, d. 1510: 27 – *All Souls College*, David Lloyde, d. 1510: 27 – *New College*, Academic dress, examples of: 27 – *New College*, Thomas Cranley, Archbishop of Dublin, d. 1417: 25 – *Thame*, Sir John Clerk, d. 1539: 29 – *Thame*, Richard Quartermayne, *c.* 1460: 25

SOMERSET: *Ilminster*, Nicholas Wadham, *c.* 1618: 31 – *Wedmore*, George Hodges, engr. *c.* 1630: 20

STAFFORDSHIRE: *Clifton Campville*, Anon. *c.* 1310 (palimpsest): 33 *Okeover*, Humphrey Oker, d. 1538 (palimpsest): 33

SUFFOLK: *Ipswich*, St Mary Tower, A notary, *c.* 1475: 24 – *Ipswich*, St Mary Quay, Thomas Pounder, d. 1525: 35, pl. 28 – *Stoke-by-Nayland*, Sir William Tendring, d. 1408: 9

SURREY: *Beddington*, Nicholas Carew, d. 1432: pl. 17 – *Stoke d'Abernon*, Sir John d'Aubernoun I, d. 1277: 10, 12, pl. 1 – *Stoke d'Abernon*, Sir John

40   d'Aubernoun II, d. 1327: 14, 15, 16 – *Walton-on-Thames*, John Selwyn, Park-keeper, d. 1587: 28

SUSSEX: *Amberley*, John Wantele, d. 1424: 28 – *Arundel*, Sir John Fitzalan, Earl of Arundel (effigy): 18 – *Cowfold*, Prior Nelond, d. 1433: 27, 30, pl. 21 – *West Firle*, Sir Edward and Lady Gage, engr. 1595: 20, pl. 12 – *Fletching*, Peter Denot, *c*. 1440: 28, pl. 31B – *Trotton*, Lady Camoys, *c*. 1310: 20

WARWICKSHIRE: *Warwick*, *St Mary's*, Sir Thomas de Beauchamp, Earl of Warwick, d. 1401: 32

YORKSHIRE: *Aldborough*, William de Aldeburgh, *c*. 1360: 17, 28 – *Aughton*, Richard Ask, d. 1460: 12, pl. 9A – *Beverley Minster*, Lady Percy, *c*. 1340: 32 – *Cowthorpe*, Brian Roucliff, d. 1494: 31 – *York Minster*, Archbishop William Grenefield, d. 1315: 25

BRASSES ON THE CONTINENT

BELGIUM: *Ghent*, William Wenemaer, d. 1325: 35

DENMARK: *Ringsted*, King Eric Menved and Queen Ingeborg, d. 1319: 34 – *Roskilde*, Duke Christopher, d. 1363: 36

FINLAND: *Nousis*, St Henry: 35

FRANCE: *Amiens*, Jean Aventage, d. 1450: 36 – *Le Mans*, Geoffrey Plantagenet, d. 1149 (enamel): 9 – *Rouen*, John, Duke of Bedford, d. 1435: 36

GERMANY: *Constance*, Robert Hallum, Bishop of Salisbury, d. 1417: 31, pl. 20 – *Lübeck*, brasses at: 35 – *Mainz Cathedral*, brasses at: 36 – *Meissen*, brasses at: 35 – *Nordhausen*, brasses at: 35 – *Verden, nr Hanover*, Bishop Yso Wilpe, d. 1231: 7, 26, pl. 32

ITALY: *Susa*: 36

PORTUGAL: *Evora*: 36

SPAIN: *Seville*, Duke of Alcalá: 36

Sir John d'Aubernoun, d. 1277,
Stoke d'Abernon, Surrey, in mail

1

Sir Roger de Trumpington, d. 1289,
Trumpington, Cambridgeshire,
in mail

2

Sir John de Creke and Lady, *c.* 1325,
Westley Waterless, Cambridgeshire,
mixed mail and plate armour

Sir Hugh Hastings, d. 1347, Elsing, Norfolk,
mail and plate (upper part)

4

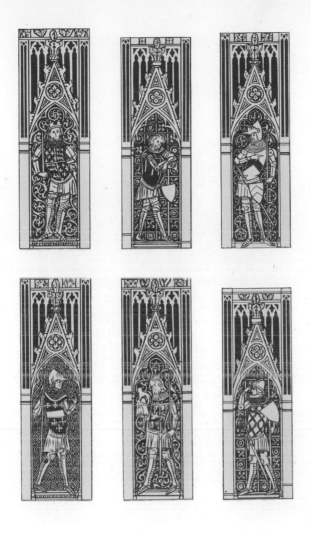

Sir Hugh Hastings, compartments of shafts, including
King Edward III and the Duke of Lancaster, Elsing, Norfolk

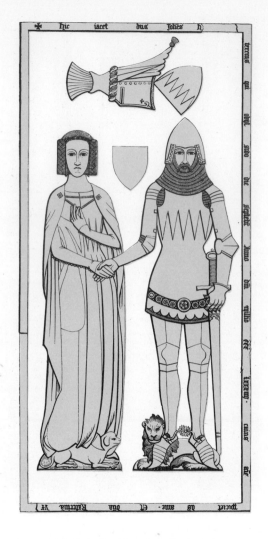

Sir John Harsick and Lady, d. 1384,
Southacre, Norfolk

6

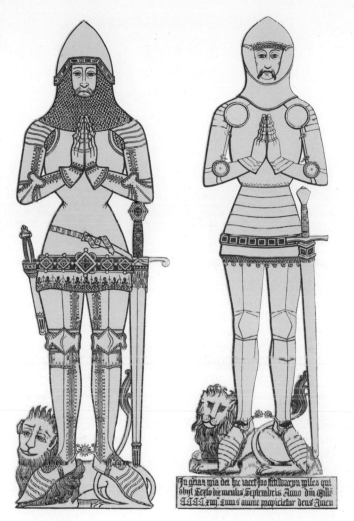

(a) A member of the Dalison
family, c. 1400, Laughton,
Lincolnshire

(b) Sir Ivo Fitzwaryn, d. 1414,
Wantage, Berkshire, complete
'white' armour

(a) John Daundelyon, 'gentilman',
d. 1445, Margate, Kent,
armour in Italian style

(b) Thomas Wayte, d. 1482,
Stoke Charity, Hampshire,
Gothic armour

(a) Richard Ask, d. 1460, Aughton,
Yorks. (Yorkshire type). Gothic
armour with sallet and beaver

(b) Edmund Clere, d. 1488,
Stokesby, Norfolk (East
Anglian Type)

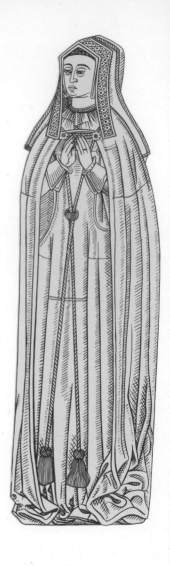

Sir Thomas Brooke, d. 1529, and Lady, Cobham, Kent

Sir Thomas Bullen, K.G., Earl of Wiltshire
and Ormonde, d. 1538 (father of
Queen Anne Boleyn), Hever, Kent

Sir Edward Gage, d. 1569, and Lady, West Firle, Sussex.
Engraved by Gerard Johnson in 1595

Sir Edward Filmer, d. 1629, and family, East Sutton,
Kent. Signed by Edward Marshall

13

Dame Joan de Cobham, *c.* 1310-20,
Cobham, Kent

14

(a) Lady Moyne, 1404,
Sawtry, Hunts

(b) Jane Keriell, d. 1455,
Ash-next-Sandwich, Kent
(Horned head-dress)

(c) Lady Say, 1473, Broxbourne,
Hertfordshire
(Butterfly head-dress)

(d) Elizabeth Perepoynt, 1543,
West Malling, Kent
(French hood)

Sir John Cassy, d. 1400, and Lady, Deerhurst,
Gloucestershire (Judge's robes)

16

Nicholas Carew, d. 1432, and Lady,
Beddington, Surrey

Wool merchant and wife, *c.* 1400, Northleach, Gloucestershire

18

Civilian and wife, *c.* 1600, Harrow, Middlesex

Robert Hallum, Bishop of Salisbury,
d. 1417, English brass in Constance Cathedral,
Germany

Thomas Nelond, Prior of the
Cluniac Priory of Lewes, d. 1433,
Cowfold, Sussex

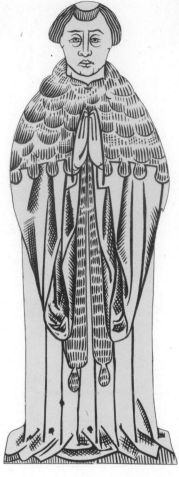

(a) John Sleford, rector, (chaplain to Queen Philippa), d. 1401, Balsham, Cambridgeshire, in cope

(b) Richard Adams, d. 1522, vicar and prebendary, East Malling, Kent, in almuce

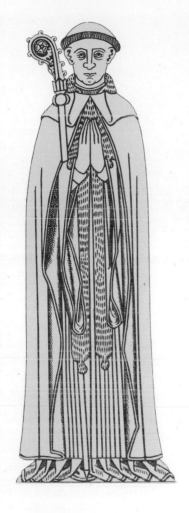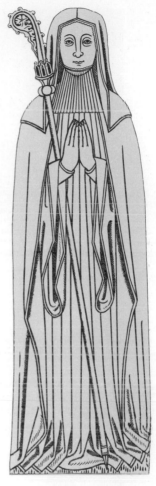

(a) Richard Bewfforest, Prior of
Dorchester, c. 1510, Dorchester,
Oxfordshire

(b) Dame Elizabeth Herwy,
Abbess of Elstow, d. 1527,
Elstow, Beds., wearing barbe

23

Portion of the brass of Adam de Walsokne, d. 13

d his wife, King's Lynn, Norfolk. Flemish brass

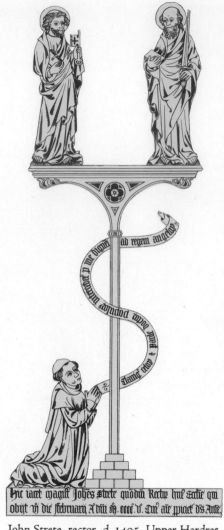

John Strete, rector, d. 1405, Upper Hardres,
Kent (Bracket brass)

Robert Paris, d. 1408, and wife, Hildersham, Cambs.
Floriated cross with Trinity

Thomas Pounder and wife, 1525, St Mary Quay, Ipswich, Suffolk.
Flemish Brass

28

Samuel Harsnett, Archbishop of York, d. 1631,
Chigwell, Essex

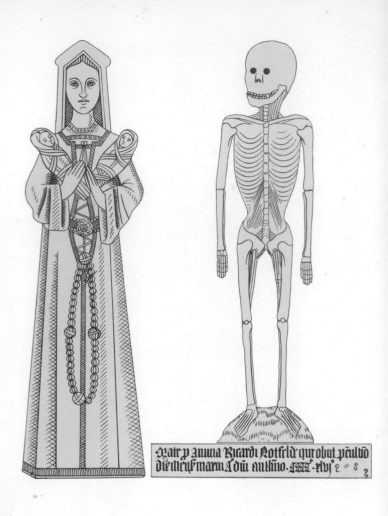

(a) Anne Astley, d. 1512,
with two chrysoms in
her arms, Blickling,
Norfolk

(b) Richard Notfelde,
d. 1446,
a skeleton,
Margate, Kent

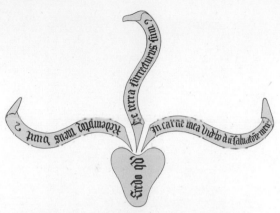

(a) Thomas Smyth, vicar, d. 1433, sacred heart, Margate, Kent

(b) Peter Denot, glover, c. 1440, Fletching, Sussex

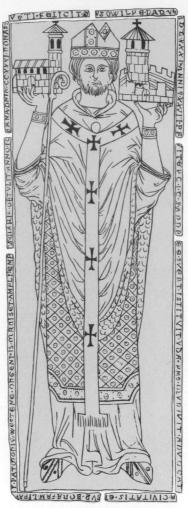

Bishop Yso Wilpe, d. 1231,
Verden, near Hanover,
Germany